Technology in the Time of
The Vikings

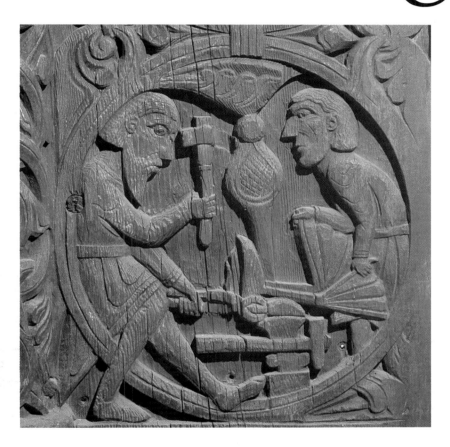

Peter Hi~~k~~

RSVP
RAINTR~~EE~~
STECK-VAU~~GHN~~
P U B L I S H~~ERS~~
The Steck-Vaughn C~~ompany~~

Austin, Te~~xas~~

Titles in the series

Ancient Egypt   **The Aztecs**

Ancient Greece   **The Maya**

Ancient Rome   **The Vikings**

Cover picture: Viking shipbuilders at work
Title page: A Viking smith working metal in his forge

Published by Raintree Steck-Vaughn Publishers,
an imprint of Steck-Vaughn Company

Library of Congress Cataloging-in-Publication Data
Hicks, Peter.
Technology in the time of the Vikings / Peter Hicks.
   p.   cm.
   Includes bibliographical references and index.
   Summary: Examines many of the technological
   innovations that the Vikings incorporated into
   their daily lives in such areas as weapons and
   armor, transportation, and jewelry-making.
   ISBN 0-8172-4880-3
   1. Vikings—Material culture—Juvenile literature.
   2. Vikings —History—Juvenile literature.
   3. Vikings—Social life and customs—Juvenile literature.
   [1. Vikings 2. Technology—Scandinavia—History.]

97-28053

he United States.
01 00 99 98

Contents

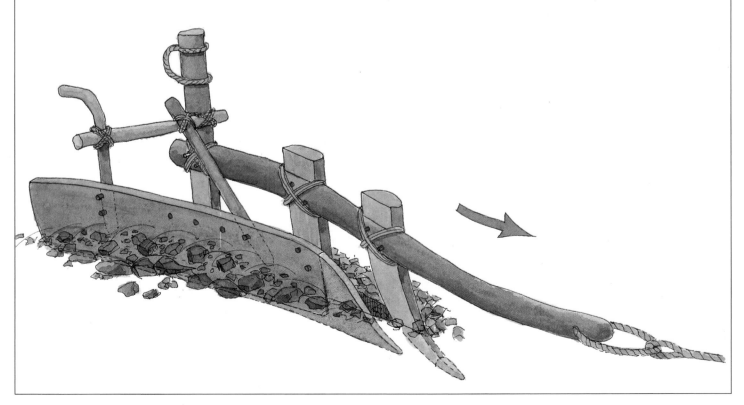

Introduction

The Vikings built ships so that they could travel along deep fjords, like this one in Norway.

In earlier times, people developed the technology they needed to help them survive. They used technology to build shelters and make clothes to protect them from harsh weather. They also used technology to help them grow enough food to beat starvation, to make war, and to travel long distances.

The Vikings were a people who lived in Scandinavia. The mountains, deep rivers, and fjords in this part of northern Europe made traveling overland very difficult. It made sense to use rivers and the seas around the coasts as routeways, and the Vikings developed their skills of shipbuilding and sea roving to allow them to do this. Their name "Viking" actually comes from the Viking word for "seafarer."

Scandinavia is close to the Arctic Circle, and it has very cold winters. The harsh climate and shortage of good, fertile land made it hard for the Vikings to grow enough food to feed their growing population. The threat of famine forced many people to leave their homeland and risk everything on a dangerous journey across the seas. From the eighth century onward, the Vikings traveled south, east, and west to take over new lands. Whenever they went into rough cold oceans or hostile lands, they relied on their technology for survival.

Leaving their homes in Norway, Denmark, and Sweden, the Vikings traveled as far as North America, North Africa, and the Middle East.

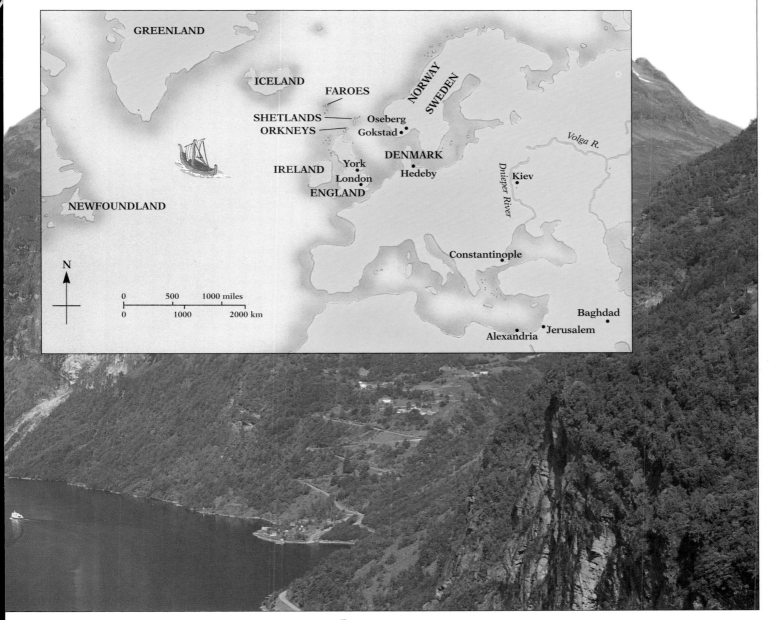

Food

Producing Food

For the Vikings, producing food was rarely easy. Some land could be cultivated, but the more northerly areas were too mountainous, rocky, and cold to grow crops. Animals could be raised there, though, and the Vikings kept cattle, sheep, and pigs. The sea, rivers, and lakes provided a constant supply of food, and the Vikings used nets or fishhooks to catch fish. Throughout the Viking world, hunting was an important way of providing more food, and there were plenty of reindeer, elk, bears, red deer, hares, and birds. The Vikings also gathered food that grew wild, such as berries and fruits, along with birds' eggs and honey from wild bees.

Before crops could be grown, woodland had to be cleared for fields. The Vikings used the "slash-and-burn" method, cutting down and then burning the trees. They dug or pulled out the roots to make the land ready to plow.

Plowing

To grow the four main cereals—rye, oats, wheat, and barley—plowing was essential. The Vikings used a basic "ard" plow. This was a pointed wooden pole—often tipped with iron—that was dragged through the soil to break it up. It often had two handles for steering and was dragged by horses or oxen. The ard worked well on light soils, but on heavier clay soils Viking farmers had to use a heavy plow, like this one.

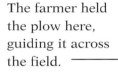

The farmer held the plow here, guiding it across the field.

The moldboard turned over the soil to make a furrow.

The plowshare lifted the soil.

The coulter broke up the soil.

Oxen were attached here.

Sowing

Once the soil had been plowed, seed was sown by the "broadcast" method: it was thrown into the furrows by hand from a sack. This unreliable method of sowing and the large numbers of weeds often made the harvests poor.

Harvesting

The Vikings used iron tools for harvesting. Although these had wooden handles to make them more comfortable to use, harvesting was always back-breaking work. The crops were cut with curved sickles or scythes, like the one shown here. The Vikings used hard, specially shaped stones called whetstones to sharpen the blades. The handle of this scythe is a modern replacement. When archaeologists find tools like this, the handles have usually rotted away.

Other Farm Tools

Where land was scarce, fields were often too small to plow. Here, the Vikings used spades and hoes to prepare the ground instead. The spades were wooden, tipped with iron "spade shoes" to strengthen them for digging. Cutting grass to make hay was an important job, as hay was a vital winter feed for the farm animals. Wooden forks and rakes were used to turn and gather up the hay. Leaf knives, which often had edges like those on a saw, were used to cut other plants for animal feed and bedding.

Preparing Food

One of the major challenges in Viking times was finding a way to preserve food supplies through the long winters. Stronger animals could be kept through the winter, but the Vikings slaughtered the weaker ones in October and preserved their meat. Both meat and fish could be salted, using salt boiled up from seawater or seaweed. They could also be pickled in salt-water. Fish, especially cod, herring, and haddock, were hung up to dry in the wind or put on racks in special huts and smoked.

Dairy produce was a very important part of the Viking diet, and archaeologists have found many churns that were used for turning milk into butter and cheeses. Butter was salted to preserve it, and milk was separated into curds and whey and used for pickling.

Boiling Food

The Vikings cooked food in a variety of ways. Boiling was often done in large cauldrons like these, hung on chains from a beam over the central hearth. The cauldrons were usually made from riveted iron sheets and were excellent for making porridge, stews, and soups. Their rounded bases allowed them to be heated on tripods as well.

The Vikings boiled food in specially constructed wood-lined pits. These pits held up to 175 gal. (450 l) of water, which was heated by dropping in stones that had been heated in a fire. Experiments have shown that this amount of water could be boiled within 35 minutes, and a large piece of meat cooked in about 3¹/₂ hours.

Roasting Meat

The Vikings built their ovens in the ground. As you can see in the picture below, they dug a hole and placed the meat inside. They packed hot stones around it and covered the hole with earth and turf. The meat was roasted and stewed at the same time. Clay ovens with shelves, which were used to cook fish, have also been found by archaeologists.

Earth and turf covering   Hot stones

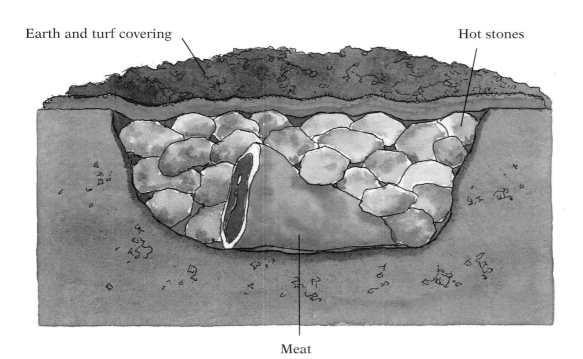

Meat

Meat was also roasted on iron spits over an open fire. The spits were either stick- or fork-shaped and often had handles. The meat was turned by hand or rested on forked sticks at either side of the fire. The Viking word for spit-roasting is *steikja*, which is where the English words "steak" and "stick" come from.

Eating and Drinking

The Vikings had two main meals a day. They ate off wooden plates or out of wooden or soapstone bowls. They cut up their meat with knives and ate it with spoons, not forks. Drinks were contained in wooden cups or drinking horns, made from the hollowed-out horns of cattle. Expensive drinking horns had metal tips and decorated rims. Because of their shape, they were impossible to put down when full, so they had to be drunk down in one swallow or passed on to a neighbor.

Making Bread

Bread was baked in all shapes and sizes, but Viking poetry mentions two types of loaf: the rough loaf, "heavy and thick, stuffed with bran," and the "thin loaves, white of wheat." Bread was an important energy food, rich in carbohydrates. However, the poisonous corncockle weed, which was harvested along with the grain, sometimes found its way into the bread and would have given the Vikings terrible stomachaches.

Grinding Flour

Once the grain had been harvested and threshed, it had to be ground into flour to make bread. For this, the Vikings used querns: two slabs of stone. The most usual type were rotary querns, with a wooden handle attached to the top stone, which was turned when grain had been placed between the slabs. The flour that was produced was rough and coarse and contained particles of grit from the querns. Excavations of Viking skeletons have shown that many people's teeth were worn down by the grit that got into the bread. Rich families could afford imported lava querns, which were finer and did not spoil the flour as much.

The rotary quern

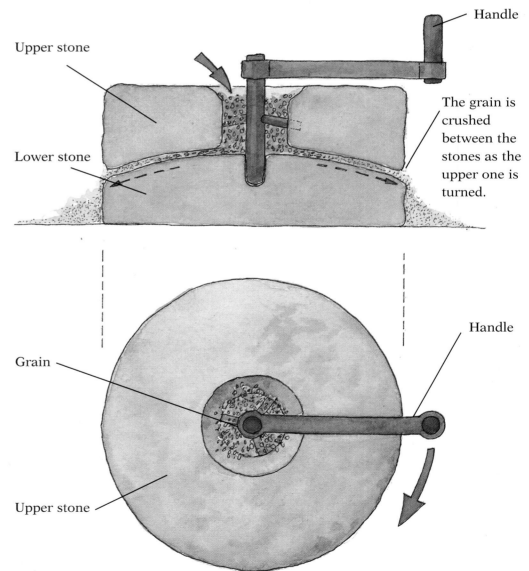

Handle

Upper stone

Lower stone

The grain is crushed between the stones as the upper one is turned.

Handle

Grain

Upper stone

Baking Bread

Small loaves and rolls were baked in ring and oval shapes. The usual way of baking bread was on round, flat pans with long handles, like the one in this picture. They were placed over the hot ashes of a fire. These pans were very similar to another cooking implement, the gridiron. Gridirons were flat, spiral strips of iron with long handles, ideal for cooking small cakes, biscuits, and cuts of meat over an open fire.

Later on, in the eleventh century, the Vikings used ovens to bake bread, instead of baking it over an open fire. The ovens were domed, with clay shelves, and were heated by a wood fire. Rakes made of beechwood were used to clean out the ash. The larger ovens were probably used by all the inhabitants in the area.

Making a Viking Recipe

You might like to try this Viking recipe for butter oat biscuits. These quantities will make about 48 biscuits. You will need to ask an adult to help you use the oven.

You will need:
3.5 oz. (100 g) butter
2 teaspoons honey
3.5 oz. (100 g) wholemeal flour
2 cups rolled oats

Preheat the oven to 350° F (180° C). Rub the butter into the flour until the mixture is the consistency of fine breadcrumbs. Mix in the oats, then stir in the honey, and mix together to form a stiff dough.

Roll teaspoons of the mixture into balls and place them on a greased baking tray, allowing room for them to spread out as they cook. Bake them for approximately fifteen minutes. Let the biscuits cool on wire trays.

Building Houses

There is no such thing as a "typical" Viking house, because designs varied throughout the Viking world, according to the location and the materials available for building. In thickly wooded areas, timber was the obvious choice. On the treeless, rocky islands of the Atlantic Ocean, builders used stone and turf. At Hedeby, a Viking town in Denmark, many buildings were built of split tree trunks, sunk into the ground next to each other. Other houses were built of wattle and daub. Their walls were made of interwoven branches—"wattle"—filled with "daub," a mixture of clay and animal dung. It was a cheap and effective way of building a simple house. Roofs varied. Some were thatched with straw or reeds, or covered with turf, while others were shingled—covered with wooden tiles, nailed to the roof frame.

A House at Hedeby

One of the houses at Hedeby has been reconstructed. It was built of wattle and daub and had four rooms. There were no load-bearing posts inside to hold up the roof, but fourteen buttresses on the outside propped up the walls to keep the weight of the roof from pushing them out. The central area around the hearth was the living area. The fire provided both heat and light, because the house did not have any windows. There was probably a hole in the roof to allow smoke to escape.

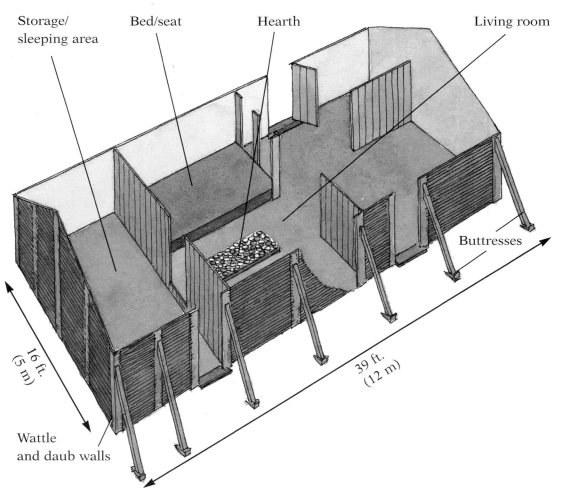

Storage/sleeping area

Bed/seat

Hearth

Living room

Buttresses

16 ft. (5 m)

39 ft. (12 m)

Wattle and daub walls

This is what the houses at Hedeby might have looked like.

The House at Stong

At a place called Stong in Iceland, a very different type of house was discovered. This diagram shows the remains of the house. It was cleverly designed to be cool in the summer, but it also gave good protection against the harsh Icelandic winters. Its dry stone walls, 4 ft. (1.3 m) thick, were covered with turf. Leading off from the main hall was the living room. A loom would have been kept here, leaning against the wall. The walls of both rooms were lined with wooden panels.

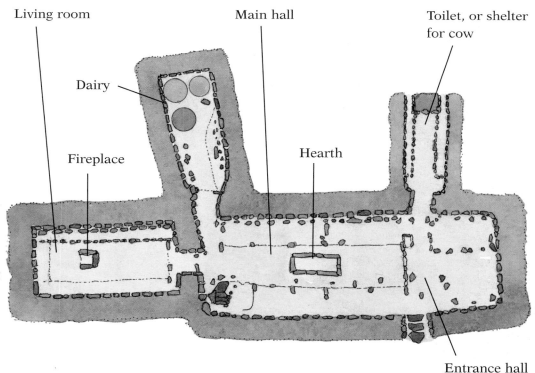

Two rooms led off from the main hall. Archaeologists think one was probably a dairy, because they found three round vat or churn marks in the floor. The other room had two drainage channels and was probably either a toilet or a place to keep a cow for milking during bad weather.

Furnishings

Most houses were not very big, so space for furniture was limited. However, the Vikings did have furniture. Large tables were set up on trestles for special occasions. Small, everyday tables have been found among the household goods that the Vikings had buried with them.

For seating, the Vikings usually used low benches set into the walls of the house. They made them by shaping low platforms out of earth and strengthening them with wooden planks and upright posts. If the benches were wide enough, they doubled as beds. The Vikings had chairs, too, and archaeologists have reconstructed a three-legged stool from pieces found in a grave.

Storage Space

The Vikings did not have cupboards. They stacked their cooking equipment on the floor or on shelves and benches. Other possessions were probably hung from the walls, beams, and rafters. They kept their valuables and prized clothing in chests. Their houses must have been very cluttered, as this reconstruction shows.

Beds

Only rich families could afford beds, which were sometimes built into the walls of the houses and partitioned off for privacy. This beautiful bed was one of the household items found buried with a ship at Oseberg in Norway. Made of carved beechwood pieces slotted into each other, it was used with mattresses and eiderdown coverings—very similar to modern comforters. Poorer Viking families slept anywhere in the house, and in winter a room with a fire was the best place. Vikings would cover themselves with furs, skins, and woolen blankets.

Lamps

Although the fire provided most light, lamps were also used. One type was a simple soapstone bowl with a wick, which was filled with oil and could have been hung from the roof. The other type, a bowl with a spiked bottom, was probably stuck in the floor. It is not known for certain if Viking houses had windows. If they did exist, they were probably "peep-holes" with shutters on the inside or pigs' bladders stretched across them.

Travel

Ships and Boats

It is because of their superb ships and their skills as sailors that the Vikings have such an important place in history. Luckily, a number of their ships have survived, and this has helped us to understand how they were built.

There were many different types of ships, all built for different purposes. Small boats were referred to by their total number of oars: a *sexaeringer,* for example, had six oars and was rowed by three men. In larger, wider ships, men could only row one oar each, sitting side by side on benches. These ships were described by their number of benches, so a "fifteen-bencher" carried thirty oars.

Viking sailors preferred coming in to land at night, but sometimes they were forced to spend nights at sea in rough weather. The T-shaped crutches on larger ships, which held the lowered yard, sail, and oars, were probably also used to support tentlike canvas shelters.

The Gokstad Ship

In 1880, a burial mound was excavated at Gokstad in Norway. Archaeologists were amazed to discover a wonderful Viking ship preserved in blue clay. It had a huge T-shaped keel and was "clinker-built": each side contained sixteen overlapping oak planks, or "strakes," riveted together to form the hull. The hull had been made waterproof with a coat of tar. The ship was a magnificent 75 ft. (23 m) long and 17 ft. (5.25 m) across. When it was empty, it weighed 9 tons, but with a crew and equipment on board this would have doubled to 18 tons.

The Construction of the Ship

The builders of the Gokstad ship used supple roots from spruce trees to lash the oak hull to the pine frames. This gave the ship great flexibility when sailing through rough seas. The builders set the pine mast, which could be raised and lowered, into a large block of oak that was fixed to the keel. The deck planks, which were also made of pine, were left loose, so that the crew could store possessions, such as clothes and weapons, in the hull. These were wrapped in skins to keep them dry. If there was no wind, the ship could be rowed, using 32 pine oars. Each oar-hole could be covered with a hinged disk when the oars were not in use.

Mast

Crutch, used to hold the sail, yard, and oars when they were not being used.

Oar-hole

Deck planks

Hull

Storage space below deck

Overlapping strakes

Frame

Keel

Steering the Ship

To steer, the Viking sailors used a large oar mounted at the back of the ship on the starboard side. (The word "starboard"— the name for the right-hand side of a ship—comes from the Viking word *styra*, which means "to steer." The oar was fastened to the ship with a piece of supple tree root, and controlled by a tiller that was slotted into the top of it. When the ship was beached, the oar could be quickly raised by unfastening the straps that held it steady against the top strake, or "gunwale."

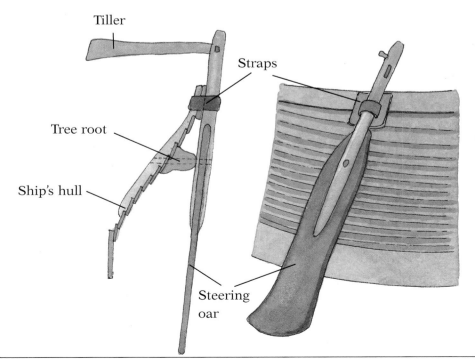

Tiller

Straps

Tree root

Ship's hull

Steering oar

Warships and Trading Ships

The most exciting collection of Viking ships found so far was discovered under water in Roskilderfjord in Denmark. There, archaeologists raised five ships that had been deliberately sunk in the eleventh century to block the harbor from attack. Two of the ships were probably warships, and the other three were cargo ships.

Viking warships had to be speedy. The narrower they were, the faster they sailed, because they produced less resistance from the water. They were often six or seven times longer than their width, which is how they became known as "longships." One of the Roskilde warships was 59 ft. (18 m) long, but only 8.5 ft. (2.6 m) wide. Fast under sail and easy to row, the longships could swiftly attack coastal settlements or towns far up rivers. The second Roskilde warship had a badly worn keel—perhaps evidence of many beachings during its life as a raider.

Cargo Ships

The Roskilde cargo ships were the first Viking ships connected with sea trade ever found. This is a reconstruction of one of them. It was a small ship, built of oak. Unlike the Gokstad ship, the strakes were not lashed to the frames but were fixed with wooden pegs called "trenails." The hold carried up to 5 tons of cargo. In rough or rainy weather, it was probably covered with animal skins, to protect the cargo inside.

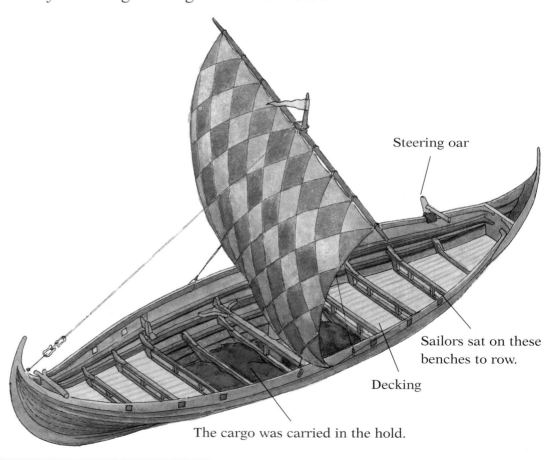

Steering oar

Sailors sat on these benches to row.

Decking

The cargo was carried in the hold.

Making a Viking Ship

You will need a piece of cardboard at least 20 in. (50 cm) x 10 in. (25 cm); two thin pieces of dowel—one about 6 in. (16 cm) long for the mast and one about 5 in. (13 cm) long for the yard; a piece of stiff paper about 5 in. (12 cm) x 5 in. (12 cm) for the sails; scissors, paints, and glue. You also need a sheet of scrap paper.

1 Draw one side of your Viking ship on the cardboard. It needs to be about 12 in. (30 cm) long. Cut it out, then draw around the shape to make the second side.

2 Glue the sides into a simple boat shape.

3 Put a piece of scrap paper over the top of the boat and draw the outline of the deck. Use this as a guide to cut the shape out of cardboard. Allow about an extra half inch all around the edge of the deck.

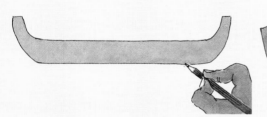

4 Paint the deck and the sides of the boat. Make small cuts around the edge of the deck shape, then turn up the edge and glue the deck into the boat. Cut a thin strip of cardboard, make a hole in the center, and fold it as shown in the diagram. Attach it to the center of the deck to hold the mast.

5 Cut out the sail, color it, and glue it onto the yard.

6 Attach the yard to the mainmast. Insert the mast into the support on the deck.

7 Cut out a steering oar and attach it to the side of the ship. You might like to add a dragon prow as well.

Making Voyages

The best account of what it was like to sail in a Viking ship came from a man named Magnus Anderson. In 1893, he sailed a replica of the Gokstad ship across the Atlantic. He wanted to remind people that it was Leif Ericsson, about A.D. 992, who had been the first European to land in North America. It took Anderson twenty-eight days to reach Newfoundland. He noticed that the ship was fast and very flexible in the face of rough, powerful waves. His greatest praise was for the steering oar, which worked well and was easy to use. "One man could steer in any weather . . ." he later wrote.

The Rigging

How were splendid ships like the Gokstad ship sailed? First, the mast had to be raised and locked into position with a block of oak. It was steadied by ropes attached to the sides of the ship, called "shrouds," and to the bow and stern by "stays." The "forestay" at the front was used to raise and lower the mast. The sail had to be large enough to catch the wind. Sails were made of a rough woolen cloth called *wadmal*, and Viking writers tell us that they were often striped or checkered. The sail was attached to a long wooden beam, called a yard, so that it could be easily hoisted up the mast. On the Gokstad ship, the yard was more than 40 ft. (13 m) long.

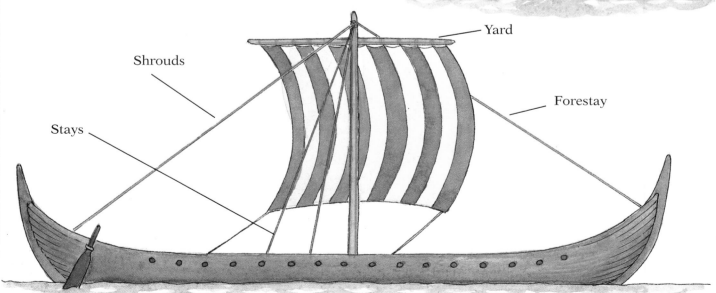

Shrouds

Stays

Yard

Forestay

Reefing the Sails

Once the sail had been hoisted, the sailors could adjust its size to suit the wind conditions. This is called "reefing." We are not sure how the Vikings did this. It is thought that a series of ropes passed through loops on the sail, and when the sailors raised or lowered the sail, they pulled or let out the ropes at the side. It was similar to letting down a modern window blind. You can see this happening in this Viking picture stone. The sail could also be shortened by lowering the yard down the mast.

Navigation

It is incredible that Viking sailors reached so many far-flung places with so little navigational equipment. A weather vane, like this one, with colorful streamers and pennants tied through the holes, was mounted on the mast and could be used to determine the wind direction. When crossing seas and oceans, the Vikings had to rely on the sun and stars to help them navigate. Sightings of groups of islands, or of seabirds and mammals, also helped them to be sure that they were going in the right direction.

Traveling Overland

Land transportation varied with the seasons. In the summer, the rich traveled by horse and the poor traveled on foot. In the winter, getting around was more difficult, and most people used skates, skis, and sleds. Although ships were very important for carrying out trade in Scandinavia, people also made long and difficult land journeys. They used packhorses, four-wheeled wagons, and large sleds with detachable boxes to carry heavy goods.

Horses were important and valuable possessions. The remains of horses have been found at burial sites, often with remnants of leather bridles still in place. Very few saddles have survived, but it appears they were made of wood and leather. Stirrups, which were often beautifully decorated, were made of iron, with rectangular hoops through which leather straps were looped. Spurs were simple—just two short, sharp points that were dug into the horse's sides. To help the horses keep their grip on snow or ice, iron spikes were attached to their feet.

The Oseberg Sled

In the Oseberg ship burial, this splendid sled was found. It is built on two runners, curved at the front. A shaft connected to the front suggests that when it was loaded the sled was pulled by animals.

The outer edge was covered with a thin metal rim.

Spoked wheels

The rims were made up of six blocks of shaped wood.

Underneath the wagon

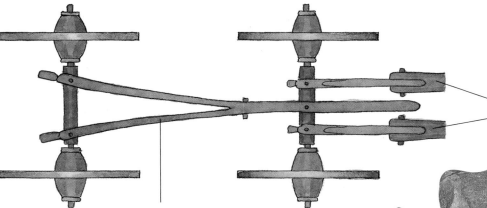

The axles were connected by a beam.

The horse was harnessed to these two shafts.

The Oseberg Wagon

A wonderful wagon was also found in the Oseberg ship burial. It was a special vehicle—perhaps the cart used to carry the body to the funeral—but it shows how everyday wagons were built. Generally, the driver perched on the edge of the wagon when it was empty and sat on the goods for comfort when it was carrying a load.

Skates

It seems that ice skates, like the ones in this picture, and skis were used widely for travel and sports. The Viking word for "skates" is *isleggr*, meaning "ice leg bone," and this is how the Vikings made their skates —from the bones of horses, oxen, or deer. They were smoothed and shaped so that they could be used to speed over frozen lakes and rivers. Skis were useful for cross-country travel in deep snow. It appears they had footrests and smoothed grooved bottoms and were used with sticks for balance.

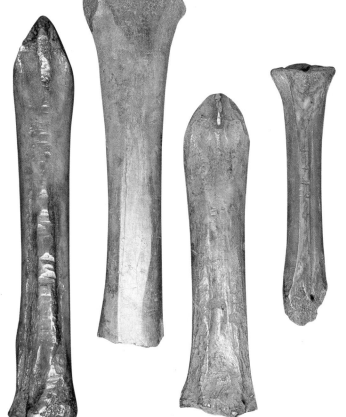

Crafts

The Ironsmith

The ironsmith was probably the most important craftsman in the Viking world. He not only made the weapons that helped Viking warriors win battles and take over other lands, but also made farm tools that helped the population feed itself. For example, the smith made the axes that were used to clear the forest and allowed land to be cultivated. There is no doubt that their skills, which were constantly in demand, gave smiths a very high status. Their skills did not come cheap: archaeologists have noticed that some of the richest Viking graves belonged to ironsmiths. Viking literature is full of stories about smiths, and the god Thor always carried a hammer —the smith's main tool.

Smelting Iron

Iron comes from iron ore, a rock that contains veins of iron. To extract the iron, the rock has to be heated to a very high temperature—2100° F (1150° C)—so that the metal in it melts. This process is called smelting. The Vikings used simple bowl furnaces, like the one shown here, to smelt iron. They were heated by charcoal and made hotter with the help of bellows. During the smelting process, all the impurities, or "slag," from the iron ore fell to the bottom of the furnace. A lump of pure iron, called a "bloom," was left. This was reheated by the smith and hammered into bars.

Waste gases escaped here.

Clay tube

Clay dome

Bellows were inserted here to pump in more air and make the fire burn more fiercely.

Pit

Clay lining

Iron ore and charcoal

The Smith's Tools

These tools, found in a smith's grave in Norway, give us a good idea of how he worked. He heated the metal until it was red-hot in his forge and then beat and shaped it.

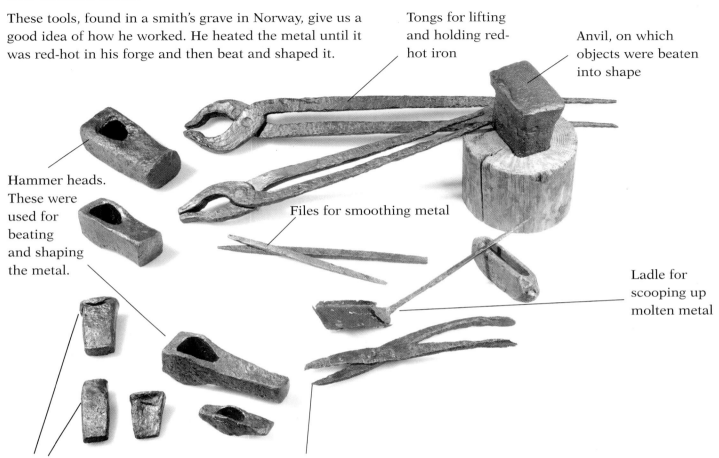

Tongs for lifting and holding red-hot iron

Anvil, on which objects were beaten into shape

Hammer heads. These were used for beating and shaping the metal.

Files for smoothing metal

Ladle for scooping up molten metal

Flatters were used to smooth and flatten the surface of the metal.

Metal shears for cutting sheet iron

A Smith at Work

Here we see a Viking smith at work in his forge. He is hammering a piece of iron, held in the firm grip of his tongs. His assistant, possibly his son, is keeping the fire hot with air from the bellows.

Viking smiths were also very skilled at making steel. This was done by adding small amounts of carbon (which is found in charcoal) to the iron. They used steel to make high-quality bladed tools, such as swords or knives.

Bone and Leather

Bone and leather were two very popular materials in the Viking world. They were tough and lasted a long time. They were also plentiful, because animals slaughtered for food provided lots of skin and bones. Antlers, which were also used, were easy to find because the deer shed them every spring.

Bone could be made into many useful things—combs, whistles, pipes, hair pins, toggles to fasten clothing, belt-ends, and ice skates. Leather was even more widely used. It was hard-wearing and flexible and could be used for clothing, belts, shoes, gloves, bridles, and scabbards for swords and daggers. The men who turned animal hides into leather were called tanners. It was their job to prepare the hides so that they would not rot. The best way they had of doing this was to soak the hides in crushed oak bark and water. It was a very smelly process, involving rotting animal flesh and fat, and it was usually carried out on the outskirts of towns.

Making a Comb from an Antler

1 The craftsman cut off the pointed "tines" of the antler, leaving the best-quality material, called the "beam," for him to work.

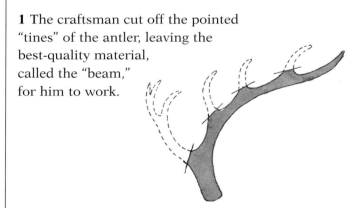

2 Using a saw, he cut a series of rectangular tooth plates from the beam.

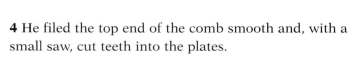

3 The craftsman attached these with two long connecting plates. These were also cut from the antler and were fastened with iron or bronze rivets.

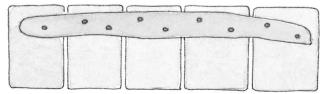

4 He filed the top end of the comb smooth and, with a small saw, cut teeth into the plates.

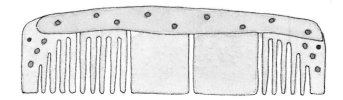

Making a Pair of Viking Shoes

Leather is a very tough material, and the Vikings needed special tools to work it. It was too hard to sew, so holes had to be punched in it first with a pointed tool called an awl. Thread could then be stitched through the holes. The Vikings usually scratched on decorations or stamped them into the leather. Some leather was even painted with attractive designs.

You might like to make some Viking shoes for yourself. You will need two pieces of felt, each approximately 12 in. (30 cm) x 12 in. (30 cm). You also need a needle, scissors, and some fine thread to sew the shoes together.

1 Take one piece of felt and stand on it. Draw around your foot and then cut out the shape. Allow about an inch extra all around so that you can sew it up later.

2 Cut out two more pieces from the felt to form each side of the upper. Make sure they are big enough to cover the front of your foot. They should meet in the middle.

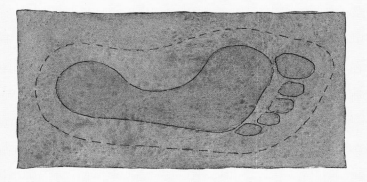

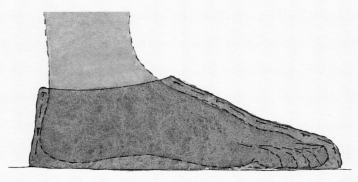

3 Pin the uppers to the sole. You might need to stuff the shoe with paper to get the shape right.

4 Stitch the shoe together using the thread. Trim off any extra material around the edges. Repeat for the second shoe, but remember to draw around the other foot this time!

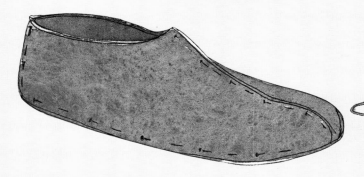

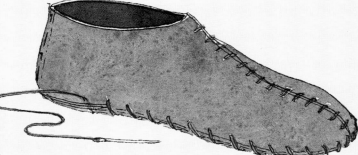

Carpentry

Viking carpenters made a huge range of wooden objects—houses, sheds, ships, boats, household goods, farm tools, wagons, sleds, and furniture. The forests of Norway, Denmark, and Sweden provided the carpenters with a plentiful supply of timber.

A Carpenter's Tools

A complete tool chest belonging to a craftsman was found in Mastermyr in Gotland, Sweden. Archaeologists believe it may have been lost when the owner was trying to cross a frozen bog in winter. Some tools were for metalworking, which suggests the owner was a general handyman. There was also a whole range of woodworking tools, including the ones shown here.

An ax was used to chop the trees down. This is called "felling."

Axes like this were used to trim the wood roughly into shape. This is called "hewing."

Auger bits, like this one, were used for boring holes. They were mounted in a T-shaped grip and twisted down into the wood.

Planks were cut into shape with saws—there were three in the chest. The longest was 20 in. (53 cm) and had sharp teeth set in groups of three or four; every second group was set in the opposite direction to give a sharp sawing edge. A rasp, or file, was used to smooth the wood.

Turning Wood

One specialist job was wood-turning. Hollow wooden objects, such
as bowls and cups, had to be made on a machine called a pole-
lathe. A roughly shaped piece of wood (called a roughout) was
fixed to a shaft, which was pinned between two supports.
A leather rope, attached to a foot pedal, was looped around the
shaft and tied to the end of a tree branch or pole. When the wood-
turner pressed the pedal, the shaft turned
quickly toward him. When he released
it, it turned away from him.

While the shaft was turning, the wood-
turner held sharp chisels or gouging
tools against the wood and gradually
shaped the object. When the bowl or cup
was finished, a core of wood was left in the
middle, attached to the shaft. This was
easily snapped off and smoothed down, and
the piece was ready to use.

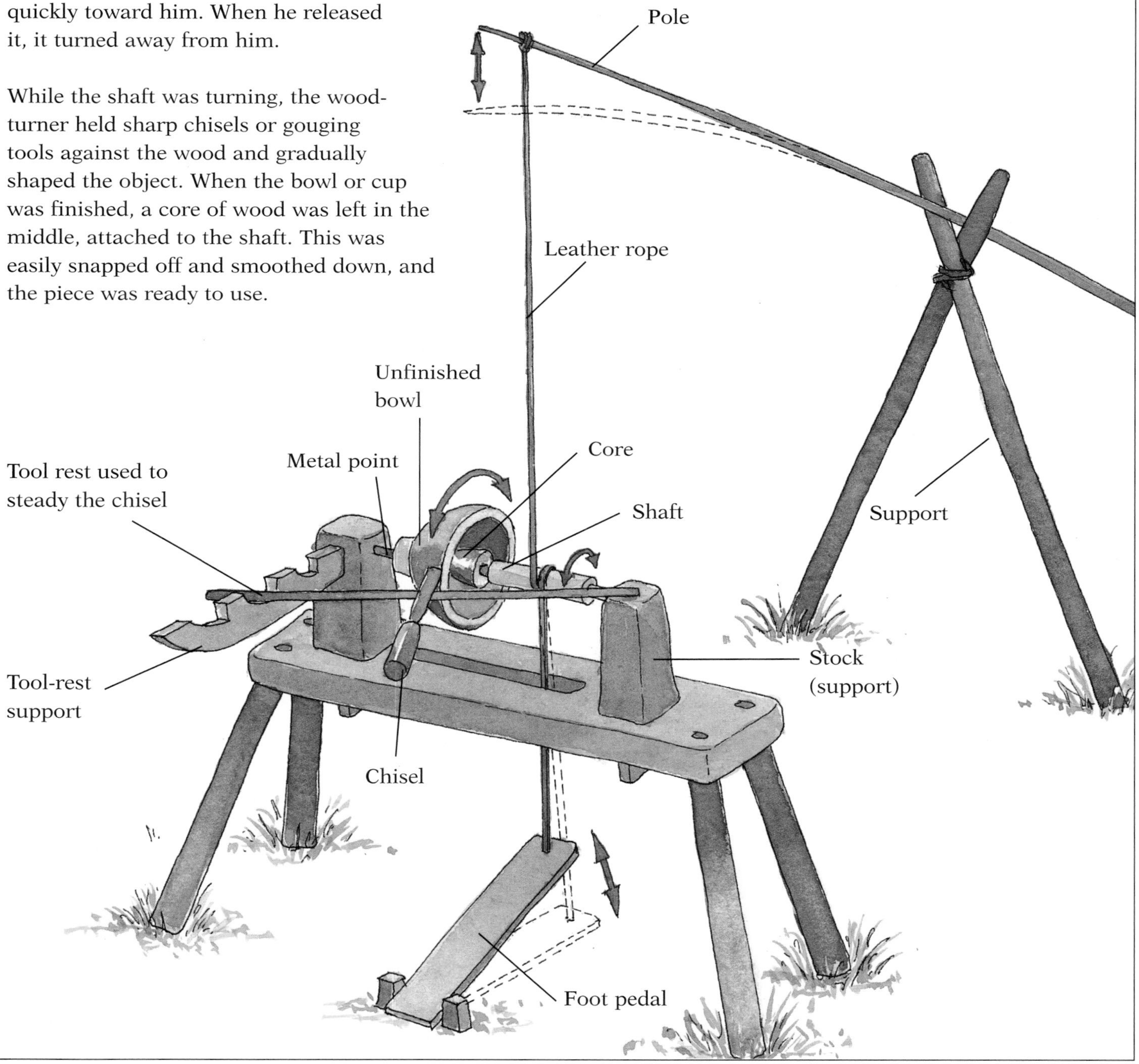

Pole

Leather rope

Unfinished
bowl

Metal point

Core

Shaft

Tool rest used to
steady the chisel

Support

Tool-rest
support

Stock
(support)

Chisel

Foot pedal

Clothing

Making Cloth

Apart from cooking, the most important job in the Viking home was weaving. In many excavated houses, evidence of looms has been found; they are usually propped up against a living-room wall. Most cloth was made from wool, but the Vikings also made linen from the fibers of the flax plant. After these have been soaked in water, they can be spun into thread. Most cloth was used to make clothes, although the Vikings also made wall hangings to decorate their houses and keep out the drafts.

Carding and Spinning

Wool was cut or pulled from sheep and goats and cleaned. It then had to be straightened or "carded," ready for spinning. To do this, the Vikings used combs with long iron prongs.

Distaff

After carding, the wool was ready for spinning. The spinner placed it on a stick called a distaff, which she held in one hand. She pulled out a strand of wool and attached it to the spindle—a smooth short stick weighted with a lump of clay or stone to help it spin. She let go of the spindle and it spun to the floor. Then she wrapped the spun wool, which is called yarn, around the spindle, and repeated the process until she had spun all the wool.

Spindle

Winding the Wool

The yarn was wound into a ball, unless it was to be dyed. Then, it was wound onto a winding reel like this instead. The winding reel was held by the crossbar, and the wool was wound from corner to corner. It was then dyed, usually with vegetable dyes. Red, green, yellow, purple, and brown were the most popular colors.

Weaving

The wool was woven on an upright loom. This was made of two wooden uprights with rests at the top to hold a circular crossbar. The warp threads—the vertical threads—were wound around this bar and weighted at the bottom with soapstone or baked-clay rings.

The weaver made sure the threads were closely woven by continually pushing the weft threads together with a flat piece of wood or a bone comb. When the cloth was taken down from the loom, it was usually shrunk in water to thicken it and close any gaps in the weave.

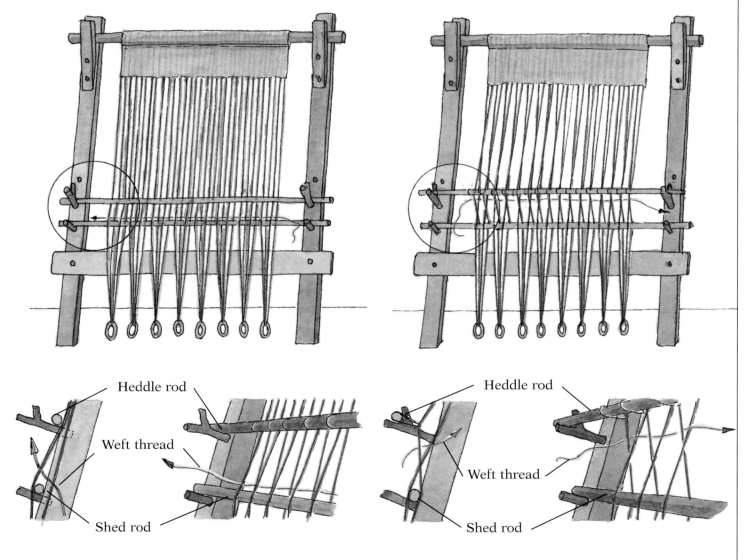

1 The weaver used a rod, called a shed rod, to separate alternate warp threads near the bottom of the loom. This made a space through which she could pass the weft (horizontal) thread.

2 The heddle rod was fastened to every other warp thread. When the weaver pulled it forward, a new space for the weft thread was created. She passed the weft thread back through this space and let the heddle rod go.

Keeping Warm

Once the wool or linen cloth had been woven on the loom, it was made into clothes, stitched together with woolen thread. Clothes were often used to show how wealthy a person was, and expensive garments were made in rich colors, with decorated borders. Poorer people, such as slaves, had to make do with very basic clothing. On top of rough woolen underclothes, Vikings usually wore a blanket, gathered at the waist, with a hole cut in the middle to push their heads through.

Footwear usually consisted of simple ankle boots. They were cut from pieces of hide, sewn together and secured by a leather lace and toggle. In summer, lower-cut, slipper-type shoes were popular. Archaeologists always used to think that the Vikings did not wear socks. However, a woolen sock was found in York. It was cleverly shaped to fit the foot and sewn by a system of loops, called *naalesbinding*.

Men's Clothes

Viking men usually wore linen shirts and long pants as underwear. Over these, they wore woven tunics—red or green were popular colors—drawn in at the middle by a belt. Trousers varied. Some were baggy and only went to the knees, and others, much more closely cut, reached to the ankles. They were held up by a belt or cord. In cold weather, fur or heavy woolen cloaks were essential, and if the cloak was not hooded, a hat was also needed. A Viking man might have worn a fur hat, a woolen or leather cap, or a simple bowl helmet. He also needed to protect his hands, with gloves or mittens of either fur or wool.

Women's Clothes

Viking women usually wore long woolen or linen shifts, which were either short-sleeved or sleeveless. Linen shifts were sometimes pleated and closed at the neck by ribbons or strings. Over the shift, a woman wore a straight woolen tunic that reached almost to the ground. It was held in place by a pair of brooches worn high on the chest. If a scarf or shawl was worn, a third brooch would have kept it secure. In winter, women probably wore stockings and linen underwear for extra warmth. Their heavy cloaks would have been similar to the men's.

Making a Viking Woman's Cap

Unmarried women wore their hair loose, but married women usually gathered theirs into a knot at the back of the neck and covered it with a woolen or silk cap. You can make a similar cap yourself.

1 Measure a rectangle of brightly colored cloth. It should be long enough to fit over your head when it is folded (see picture 4 below). Cut it out.

2 Fold the rectangle in half. With the folded edge at the top, stitch the pieces together up the right-hand edge.

3 Stitch a ribbon to each corner on the left-hand side.

4 Place the cap over your head with the ribbons at the front and tie them together.

Health and Hygiene

We know that doctors were important people in the Viking world, and that they received a good income for tending the sick and injured. Viking laws tell us that if someone was injured in a fight, he would receive compensation for the wounding. The person who had injured him would have to pay for the doctor as part of his punishment. A "full wound" was one that needed "ointment and bandage, linen, and doctor's fee."

Viking doctors knew how to lance boils, clean wounds, and stop bleeding by using hot irons (the name for this treatment is "cauterizing," and it is still used today). They applied herbal ointments to injuries and used linen bandages to keep dirt from getting into wounds. They were able to set broken limbs with bandages and wooden splints. Some of their methods seem harsh by our standards, but they were obviously skilled at even serious injuries. The warlike society in which they lived provided them with plenty of opportunities to practice!

The Onion Treatment

If a person received a wound to the intestines in a battle or fight, the Vikings had a smart way of finding out its seriousness. The patient's wound was cleaned with hot water and bandaged. Then a herbal porridge with onions was prepared, which the patient had to eat. If, after a while, the smell of onions came from the wound, it meant that the intestines had been severed and the patient would die of infection. Such an injury was known as the "porridge illness."

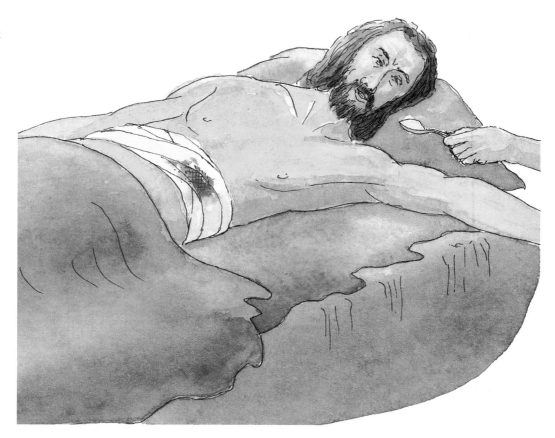

The Isolation Treatment

An Arab traveler named Ibn Fadlan, who met Vikings in Russia, wrote about their customs. He tells us that if a Viking became ill, he was put in a tent on his own with a supply of bread and water. He was not visited or spoken to until he either recovered or died. This may have been an early example of isolating an infectious person!

Keeping Clean

We do not know for sure what Viking standards of hygiene were like. Ibn Fadlan was horrified by the Vikings' washing habits and called them "the filthiest of God's creatures." However, Viking poetry tells us that guests seated at tables must receive "water, a towel, and a hearty welcome." Vikings who settled in England were praised for combing their hair, bathing on Saturdays (which was known as *laugardayr*, or "bathday"), and changing their underwear regularly. On the other hand, it was usual to wash rough clothes in cow urine because the ammonia in it helped to get them clean!

Many bone combs, like this one in its case, have been found all over the Viking world. The Vikings certainly seem to have taken a lot of trouble over their hair, but lice and fleas would have been a constant problem.

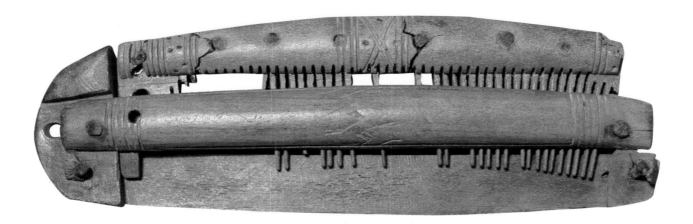

Jewelry

Working Metal

In Viking times, men and women wore a lot more jewelry than they do today. Brooches, pendants, necklaces, finger-rings, arm-rings, earrings, buckles, belt-ends, and pins were beautifully decorated and made from a wide range of materials. The most popular materials for making jewelry were copper, bronze, pewter, brass, silver, gold, amber, and jet. How were these beautiful objects made?

Making Jewelry

Copper was a popular metal for making jewelry because it shone brightly and was fairly cheap. Before a craftsman could begin shaping the copper, he first had to melt it in a stone or clay cup called a crucible. At this point, he could add a small amount of tin to make bronze, which was much stronger than copper, or a little zinc, to make brass. Brass was popular because it shone like gold. The next step was to shape the metal in a mold. Molds were sometimes cut into blocks of stone or antler, but were made mostly from clay.

1 The craftsman carved the shape of the jewelry into a piece of wood.

2 Then he pressed the wood into wet clay. The clay was fired in a kiln to make it into a tough mold, which could be used over and over again.

3 With a pair of tongs, the craftsman carefully poured molten metal from a crucible into the mold.

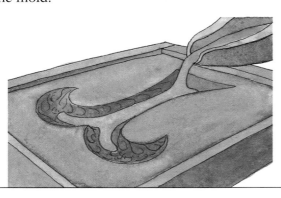

4 He waited patiently while the metal cooled and then tipped out the object or broke open the mold. If the cast was incomplete —which often happened—the piece would be melted down again. However, if it was good enough, the craftsman smoothed it with a file and then polished it.

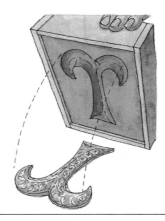

Lost-wax Casting

Metal figures like this were made by the "lost-wax" method. The craftsman made a figure from beeswax and covered it in damp clay to form a mold. When the clay had dried, he heated the mold. The wax inside it melted and ran out through a hole in the clay, leaving the mold empty. Molten metal was then poured in. When it had solidified, the craftsman broke open the mold to reveal the figure inside.

Making Rings and Bracelets

Arm-rings, finger-rings, and bracelets were made in a very skillful way. The metal was first heated and cast into narrow ingots. The craftsman then reheated an ingot until it was red-hot and forced it through a hole in an iron plate. He used tongs to stretch the ingot, making it much thinner. The process was repeated, using a series of narrower holes until the metal became wire of the required width. Then the craftsman trimmed the wire and carefully bent it into circles or spirals. These silver rings are made of twisted metal wire.

Working Amber and Jet

Pendants, beads, and rings made from amber and jet were highly valued by the Vikings. Amber, the fossilized resin of pine trees, is almost transparent and is an attractive yellow or gold color. The Vikings found it on the shores of the Baltic Sea and used it widely.

Jet is a shiny, deep-black, fossilized material, found around the world in small quantities. As well as using jet for beads and pendants, the Vikings also used it as an inlay material. Pieces of jet were fitted into sockets in pieces of metal jewelry, and molten tin was then usually used to hold the jet inlay in place. Fragments of jet jewelry have been discovered in many parts of the Viking world, especially in Norway.

Making Amber Jewelry

To make a pendant, the craftsman cut a lump of amber with a saw, drilled a hole for it to be threaded, then polished it with wet sand. Beads were much more difficult to make, because they are round. Again, the first stage was to cut a block of amber and drill a hole through it. It was mounted on a bow lathe and, while one craftsman turned the lathe, another used sharp tools to shape the bead. It was then polished. Rings were made in the same way, although a larger block of amber was used. It was sawed into slices and chiseled into a circular shape before being worked on the bow lathe.

The Bow Lathe

When the bow is pushed back and forth, it turns the shaft very quickly. The block of amber attached to the shaft turns, too, and the craftsman shapes it with sharp tools.

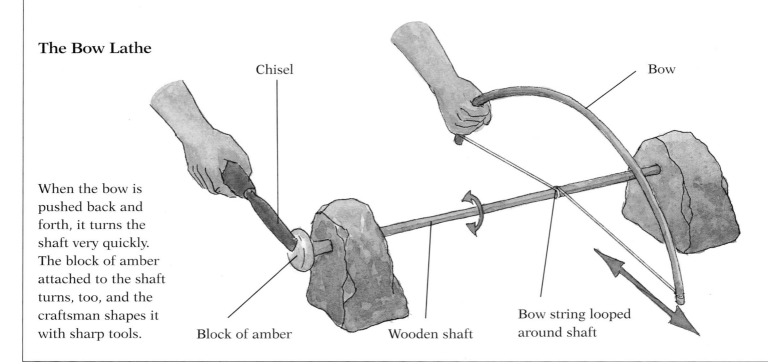

Chisel

Bow

Block of amber

Wooden shaft

Bow string looped around shaft

Making an Amber Necklace

To make a Viking-style necklace, you will need paper, 8 to 10 toothpicks, some paints, scissors and brushes, varnish, a needle, and some thread.

1 Cut out 8 to 10 long strips of paper, making them all different widths.

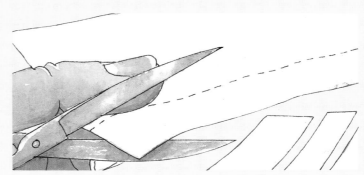

2 Take a strip of paper and spread some glue over one side. Roll the paper around a toothpick two or three times. Then take the paper off the stick and keep rolling it by hand. Roll up each strip of paper in the same way.

3 Put the strips back on the toothpicks and paint them in shades of yellow, gold, and light brown. When they are dry, give them a thin coat of varnish.

4 String the "beads" onto thread to make your necklace.

Weapons and Armor

Warriors

The most prized possessions of Viking men were their weapons. They were considered to be so important that there were laws stating the weapons each man had to own. In general, he was expected to own a sword or an ax, a spear, a bow and three dozen arrows, an iron hat, and, if possible, a protective mail shirt. They were expensive items, but a famous Viking poem tells us why they were so important:

> A man should never be more than an inch from his weapons when out in the field,
> For he never knows when he will need his spear.

In other words, a Viking warrior was expected to be ready to fight and hunt at any time. His weapons were produced by the ironsmith to a very high standard.

Bows and Arrows

Bows and arrows were widely used both in battle and for hunting. Arrows were carried in cylindrical quivers, and some of their remains have been found by archaeologists. Only the iron arrowheads, like the ones in this picture, have survived, because the shafts were made of wood, which rots easily. The arrowheads were usually leaf-shaped and had sharp spikes that were driven into the wooden shafts. They varied in length from 4 to 6 in. (10 to 15 cm), which means they were able to penetrate armor easily. A huge long bow made of yew, which must have fired arrows with tremendous force, was discovered at Hedeby in Denmark.

Making Swords

The sword was by far the most important Viking weapon. The very best blades were "pattern-welded," that is, made up of a number of individual iron strips that were twisted and then welded together. The smith could take up to a month to weld the different strips of metal into one sword. The sword was hammered very precisely to take out impurities, which would have weakened the metal and caused it to shatter on impact. Viking swords were very flexible. A blade made of steel had a very tough, sharp cutting edge.

Spears

There were two types of Viking spears: one was for throwing and the other was a hand spear, for thrusting in battle. In general, the thrusting spears had broader blades, which were often highly decorated with designs worked in silver. Throwing spears were much more slender. The iron blades were beaten into shape by the smith and had a socket for the shaft. Once the shaft had been inserted into the socket, it was riveted on.

Sword Handles

The sword blade had a tang, or sharp point, onto which the handle was fitted. The handle had three parts—the guard, grip, and pommel. The grip, usually just wider than the width of a man's hand, was made of wood, metal, or bone and sometimes had a stitched leather cover. The guard, to protect the hand, was usually a straight, short metal bar. The pommel was either a short bar or rounded D-shaped piece of metal.

Axes

The other main weapon of attack was the double-handled ax. Viking warriors often used to swing this fearsome weapon around their heads as they attacked. The shape of the ax-head varied, but a broad ax with a wide curving edge was the most popular. The cutting edge was often made of specially hardened iron, which was welded onto the main part of the ax-head.

Protection in Battle

This shield was found at Gjermundbu in Norway.

In most battles, the Vikings fought hand to hand. Because of this, defensive equipment, such as shields, mail shirts, and helmets, was very important. Shields were usually round and made up of wooden planks, bound at the edges by a riveted leather border. Warriors often locked their shields together to form a "shield-fort" around a leader or chief. Sometimes, a whole army might defend itself behind a shield wall. This would have been very effective against arrows or blows from axes and swords.

The design of helmets varied. Some were just basic iron hats, perhaps with a riveted nose guard. As a general rule, the more expensive the helmet, the more protection the head and neck received. An idea of what the Viking warriors must have looked like is given in this ancient Irish saying: "One of the hardest men to talk to is a Viking in his armor."

Making a Shield

You will need some large sheets of thick cardboard, a round plastic container, glue, scissors, masking tape, paints, and brushes.

1 Cut out a large circle from a sheet of thick cardboard.

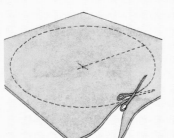

2 Cut wide strips of cardboard for the "planks" and stick them to the front of the shield.

3 Stick the margarine pot in the center of the shield at the front. This is the boss that would have protected the warrior's hand.

4 Paint the shield and boss in bright colors. You could give the shield a brown border, like the leather border on a real shield.

5 Cut a strip of cardboard and stick it to the back of the shield to make the handle.

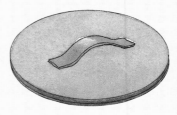

Mail Shirts

This is a helmet and the remains of a mail shirt. Mail shirts covered the body from the upper arms to the thighs with a protective coat of interlocking iron rings. Although heavy, and warm to wear in summer battles, they were excellent at protecting the wearer from glancing sword blows. However, they were no match for a speeding arrow. Only wealthy warriors could afford mail shirts—the time it took the smith to make them made them very expensive.

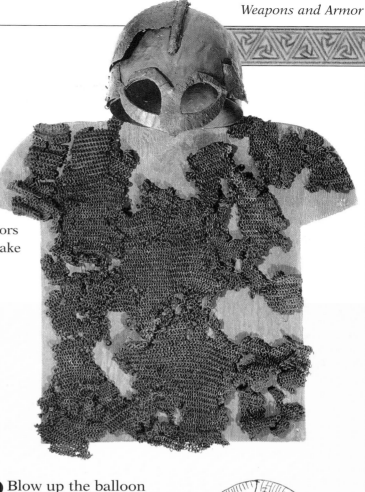

Making a Viking Helmet

You will need a balloon, wallpaper paste, newspaper, scissors, paint brushes, and some gold or silver paint.

1 Make some papier-mâché by tearing the newspaper into pieces about 1 sq. in. (8 sq. cm) and soaking it in wallpaper paste.

2 Blow up the balloon until it is slightly larger than your head. Cover it with several layers of papier-mâché and let it dry—this will take about 48 hours.

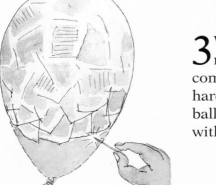

3 When the papier-mâché is completely dry and hard, pop the balloon inside it with a pin.

4 Trim the papier-mâché shell to match the shape of the helmet at the top of this page. Cut out eyes and a nose piece. Paint the helmet gold or silver.

Technology Through Time

The Vikings did not write down when they invented a new form of technology, so archaeologists have to work like detectives, piecing together evidence. Excavations of Viking settlements, discoveries like the ships at Roskilderfjord, and Viking burial sites all provide clues, but it is usually difficult to figure out exactly when a house or ship was built. Scientific methods, such as carbon dating, or the discovery of new evidence can sometimes help archaeologists date the items they find more precisely.

c. A.D. 700–800	Warships are developed, allowing the Vikings to raid neighboring countries. The technique of reefing sails is developed. Vikings from Norway settle in Orkney and Shetland. The simple ard plow is in use.
793–5	Vikings attack Lindisfarne and Jarrow in northeast England and Iona in Scotland.
795	Vikings carry out raids near Dublin, Ireland.
799	Southwestern France is attacked by Vikings.
c. 800	The ship found in the burial at Oseberg is built around this time.
c. 800–900	Wattle and daub homes are built at Hedeby in Denmark.
835 – *c.* 860s	Vikings attack England.
840	Dublin becomes a Viking base.
845	Vikings burn Hamburg in Germany.
860s	The Vikings reach Russia, North Africa, and Italy.
867	The city of York in northern England is captured by Vikings.
885	Paris is besieged by Vikings.

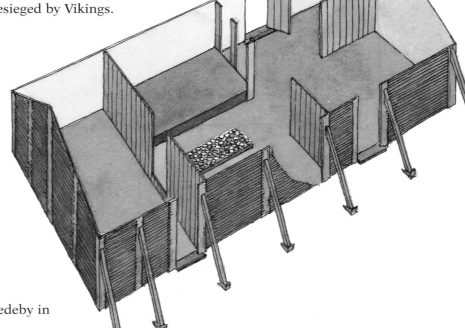

Houses like this were built at Hedeby in Denmark in the ninth century.

886	England is split up, with an area of eastern England—the Danelaw—under Viking rule.
late 800s	The Gokstad ship is built.
c. 900s	Houses made of horizontal planks are built at Jorvik (York) in England. Farmhouses like the one at Stong in Iceland are built. The grave of the ironsmith found at Bygland Morgedal in Norway (see p 25) dates from this time.
911	Vikings capture Normandy, in northwest France.
972	Vikings seize Novgorod, in Russia.
985	Erik "the Red" leads the Viking settlement of Greenland.
986	Viking seafarers sight North America.
992	Vikings set up a base in Newfoundland, in North America.
late 900s	Soapstone becomes an important material, for making bowls and other household items.
c. 1000	Plows with moldboards are in use.
1064	Denmark and Norway become separate states.
1066	Harold Hardrada, King of Norway, is killed in England at the Battle of Stamford Bridge. The Normans invade England.

The Vikings were so skilled at
shipbuilding and seafaring that they
were able to cross the Atlantic and
reach North America.

Glossary

Ammonia A chemical found in urine.

Bellows A leather bag that can be squeezed to blow air into a fire and make the fire burn more fiercely.

Charcoal Wood that has been partially burned in a special way, for use as a fuel.

Cultivated Used to grow crops.

Curds and whey Substances that form when milk clots. The curds are solid and the whey is a liquid.

Environment The surroundings in which people live.

Fjords Long, narrow inlets of the sea between high cliffs.

Forge The fire used by a smith for heating metal, or the place where a smith works.

Hearth The part of a room where the fire is made.

Hull The main part of a ship.

Ingots Blocks of cast metal.

Keel A piece of wood running along the length of a ship, to which the other main parts of the structure are attached.

Kiln A furnace for firing clay.

Loom A machine used to weave cloth.

Navigation Working out the position of a ship and the direction it needs to travel to make a journey.

Pewter A mixture of tin and lead.

Pickled Preserved in liquid.

Preserve To stop food from going bad by treating it in some way, such as by salting it or smoking it.

Rafters The wooden beams that form the framework of a roof.

Resin A sticky liquid that oozes from the bark of some trees.

Scabbards Holders for swords or daggers, usually made of leather.

Shifts Plain dresses worn as underwear.

Strakes Planks that form the sides of a ship.

Threshed When ears of wheat or barley are hit to separate the grain from the stalks.

Timber The word used to describe wood when it is used as a building material.

Yard The long plank of wood to which a sail is fastened.

Further information

Books to Read

Caselli, Giovanni. *A Viking Settler* (Everyday Life of). New York: Peter Bedrick Books, 1991.

Clare, John D. *Vikings* (Living History). San Diego: Harcourt Brace, 1992.

Hook, Jason. *The Vikings* (Look Into the Past). Austin, TX: Thomson Learning, 1993.

Margeson, Sue. *Viking* (Eyewitness Guides). New York: Dorling Kindersley, 1994.

Martell, Hazel Mary. *The Vikings* (Worlds of the Past). Parsippany, NJ: Silver Burdett Press, 1992.

————. *Everyday Life in Viking Times* (Clues to the Past). Danbury, CT: Franklin Watts, 1994.

Morley, Jacqueline. *How Would You Survive as a Viking?* Danbury, CT: Franklin Watts, 1995.

Wright, Rachel. *Vikings* (Craft Topics). Danbury, CT: Franklin Watts, 1993.

Picture acknowledgments

The publishers would like to thank the following for allowing their photographs to be used in this book: Ancient Art & Architecture Collection 14/Ronald Sheridan; Bruce Coleman 4–5/Hans-Peter Merten; C.M. Dixon *title page*, 8, 13, 21 (top), 25, 28; Michael Holford 7 (top), 9, 37 (lower); Universitetets Oldsaksamling, Oslo 7 (lower)/Ove Holst, 11/Ove Holst, 15/Kojan og Krogvold, 22/Eirik Irgens Johnsen, 25/Ove Holst, 31, 42/L. Pedersen, 43/Ove Holst; Werner Forman Archive *cover*, 16/Viking Ship Museum, Bygdoy, 21 (lower)/Statens Historiska Museum, Stockholm, 37 (top)/Thjodminjasafn, Reykjavik, Iceland; York Archaeological Trust 23, 35, 40, 41. Cover artwork is by Christa Hook.
Illustrator: Tim Benké

Index

Page numbers in **bold** indicate that there is information about the subject in a photograph or diagram.